Measure It with Math!

MEASURING AREA

T0027067

Anne O'Daly

PowerKiDS press

Published in 2024 by The Rosen Publishing Group, Inc.
2544 Clinton Street, Buffalo, NY 14224

Portions of this work were originally authored by Chris Woodford and published as *Area*.
All new material this edition authored by Anne O'Daly.

Children's Publisher: Anne O'Daly
Design Manager: Keith Davis
Picture Manager: Sophie Mortimer

Picture credits:
Key: t = top, tr = top right, b = bottom
Front Cover: Shutterstock: Svjatoslav Andreichyn r, Dima Sidelnikov l, Africa Studio tl,
Anton Prado PHOTO tr.
Interior: iStock: AJ Watt 7; NASA: Earth Observatory/JPL/Jessie Allen and
Robert Simmon 27, Goddard Space Flight/ Jeff Schmaltz, MODIS Rapid Response
Team 13; Shutterstock: 28, 24K-Production 20, Christian Bertrand 15, Blue Planet Studio 11, ClassicVector 4, Fishman64
18, Sam Foster 12, GizemG 25, Grindstone Media 8, Philip Lange 5,
Stephane Legrand 24, Oksana Mizina 19, New Africa 23, Nordroden 1, 22, Leon Rafael 21t, REDPIXEL.PL 26, Sunlight
Arrow 16, Khon Supan 10.

All other artworks and photographs © Brown Bear Books.

Cataloging-in-Publication Data

Names: O'Daly, Anne.
Title: Measuring area / Anne O'Daly.
Description: New York : Powerkids Press, 2024. | Series: Measure it with math! | Includes glossary and index.
Identifiers: ISBN 9781642827736 (pbk.) | ISBN 9781642827743 (library bound) | ISBN 9781642827750 (ebook)
Subjects: LCSH: Area measurement--Juvenile literature. | Weights and measures--Juvenile literature. |
Measurement--Juvenile literature. | Mathematics--Juvenile literature.
Classification: LCC QC104.5 O34 2024 | DDC 516'.154--dc23

Manufactured in the United States of America

CPSIA Compliance Information: Batch #CSPK24. For further information contact Rosen Publishing at 1-800-237-9932.

Find us on

Contents

What Is Area?

Imagine you want to paint the walls of your bedroom. How much paint will you need? You can figure this out if you know the size of the walls. The space inside a flat shape is its area. A big wall has a larger area than a small wall.

Measuring Area

To figure out the area of a wall, you need to know its length and its height. The length is the distance across the wall, from side to side. The height is the distance from the floor to the ceiling. The area is the length times the height.

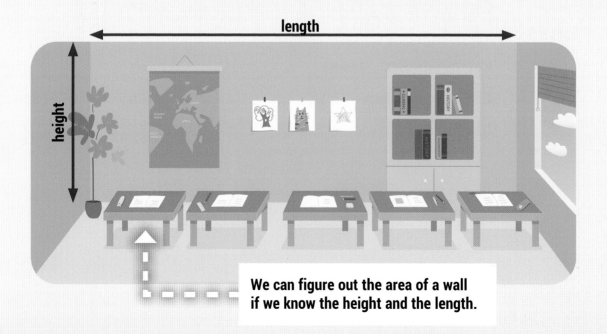

We can figure out the area of a wall if we know the height and the length.

Around the Outside

What if you wanted to measure the distance around the outside of one of the walls? That measurement is called the perimeter. The larger the wall, the larger its perimeter will be.

AREA AND PERIMETER

A rectangle has four sides and four right angles. We find a rectangle's area and perimeter if we know the length and the width.

The area is the length times the width.

6 x 10 = 60

The perimeter is the distance all the way around the rectangle. We find it by adding together all the lengths.

Perimeter = 6 + 6 + 10 + 10 = 32

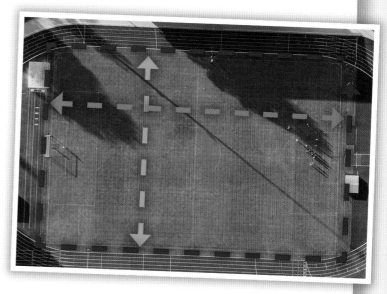

length → width → perimeter →

Measuring Squares

All measurements have their own kind of units. We measure lengths with units such as inches, feet, and yards. Areas are measured in a different way. Their measurements are called square units.

Units of Area

Suppose the floor of a room is covered with square titles. Each tile is 1 foot wide and 1 foot long. We can say that the area of each title is 1 foot by 1 foot. There is a shorter way to describe the area. We say it is 1 square foot. A square foot is a measurement of area.

TRY THIS

MEASURE A FLOOR

Each tile is 1 foot by 1 foot. If you want to put a rug on part of the floor, how big should the rug be? The part you want to cover is five tiles long and four tiles wide. What is the area of that part of the floor?

The whole floor is eight tiles wide and eight tiles long. What is the area of the whole floor?

Answers on page 32.

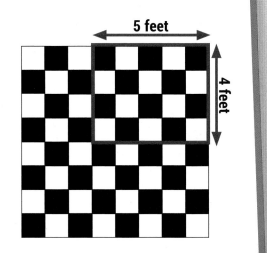

5 feet

4 feet

LENGTH AND AREA

A small increase in length can make a big increase in area. Suppose a floor has tiles that are 1 foot by 1 foot. You want to measure an area that is two tiles long by two tiles wide. How would you figure it out?

Area = 2 feet x 2 feet = 4 square feet

Now you want to measure a part of the floor that is four squares long by four squares wide.

Area = 4 feet x 4 feet = 16 square feet

Doubling the length makes the area four times bigger.

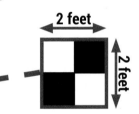

Area: 2 x 2 = 4 square feet

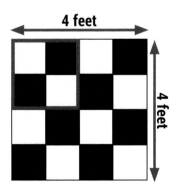

Area: 4 x 4 = 16 square feet

Measure in Metric

We can use metric units, such as centimeters and meters, to measure length. There are metric units to measure area, too. Metric units include square centimeters, square meters, and square kilometers.

We use different units for different sizes.

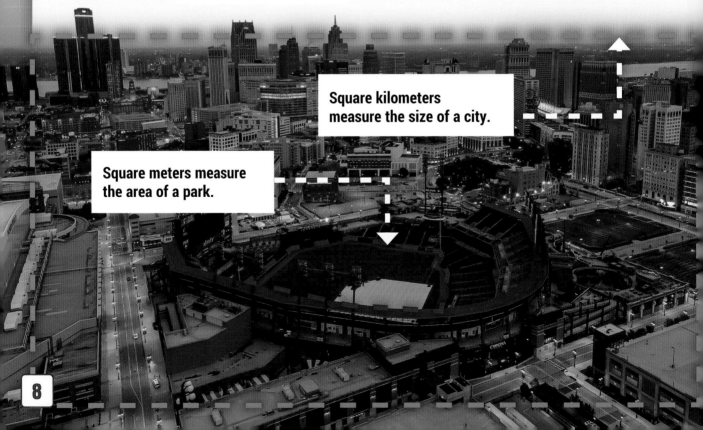

Square kilometers measure the size of a city.

Square meters measure the area of a park.

IMPERIAL AND METRIC

We can change imperial to metric measurements.
We can change metric measurements to imperial.

IMPERIAL TO METRIC
1 square inch = 6.5 square centimeters
1 square foot = 930 square centimeters
1 square yard = 0.8 square meter
1 square mile = 2.6 square kilometers

METRIC TO IMPERIAL
1 square centimeter = 0.1 square inch
1 square meter = 1.2 square yards
1 square kilometer = 0.4 square mile

Units Matter
Square centimeters measure small things. You could use square centimeters to measure the pages of this book. Square meters measure the size of your classroom, your school yard, or a sports field.

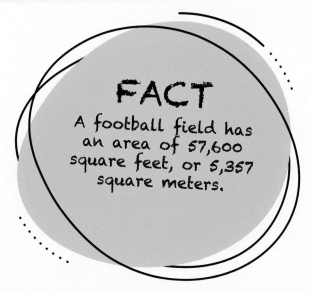

FACT
A football field has an area of 57,600 square feet, or 5,357 square meters.

Big and Small Areas

Square feet and square meters are good for measuring the area of a room. Smaller areas can be measured in square inches or square centimeters.

TRY THIS

MEASURE AN AREA

Area of this hand is 6 square inches.

A room is 10 feet x 15 feet. **What is its area?**

This book is 8 inches x 8 inches. **What is the area of one page?**

Answers on page 32.

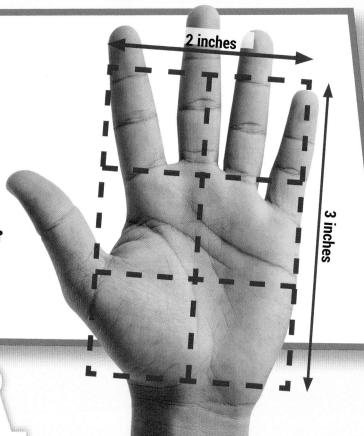

2 inches

3 inches

Very Big Areas

Larger areas are measured in square yards or square miles in the imperial system. They are measured in square meters or square kilometers in metric. People use square miles and square kilometers to measure the area of a city or a country.

The world's largest city by area is Tokyo, Japan. It measures 3,300 square miles (8,547 square km).

Measuring Land and Water

Land is measured in units called acres. An acre is the same as 43,560 square feet. It is about three-fourths the size of a football field. In the metric system, land is measured in hectares. A hectare is 100 meters by 100 meters. One hectare is about 2.5 acres.

The area of a farmer's field could be as much as 30 or even 100 acres. Can you work out the area of the field marked on this photograph, in square feet?

400 feet

900 feet

900 feet

400 feet

AREA OF WATER

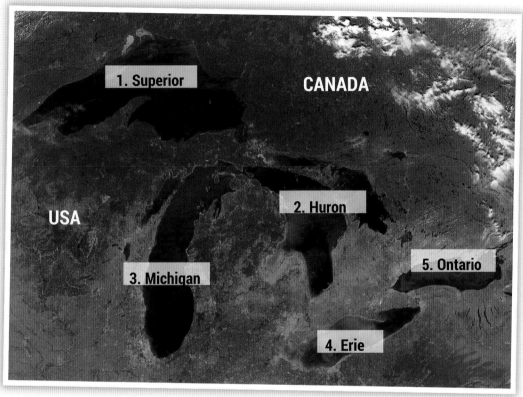

Acres can be used to measure areas of water as well as land. The biggest areas of water in North America are the Great Lakes. Each lake covers a huge area that is the same size as millions of football fields!

Lake	Area (square miles)	How many football fields?
1. Superior	31,700	15 million
2. Huron	23,000	11 million
3. Michigan	22,300	11 million
4. Erie	9,910	5 million
5. Ontario	7,550	4 million

Measuring Simple Areas

It's easy to find the area of simple shapes. The area of a square or rectangle is its length time its height. A square is a kind of rectangle. Its sides are all the same length, and it has four right angles.

A parallelogram is a four-sided shape with two parallel sides. Parallel lines are the same distance apart along their whole length. A parallelogram's area is its length times its height.

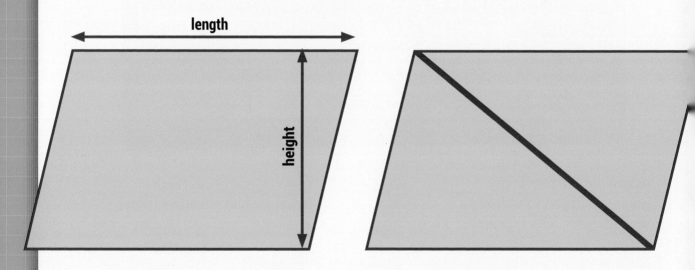

This is a parallelogram. The area of a parallelogram is its length times its height.

Two identical triangles put together make a parallelogram.

COUNTING A CROWD

How can we count the number of people in a big crowd? Counting them one by one would take a long time! It's quicker to use area. Say one person takes up 4 square feet of ground, and the total area of the place is 8,000 square feet. Dividing the total area by the area each person takes up tells us how many people are there. In this case, it is 8,000 divided by 4. There are 2,000 people in the crowd.

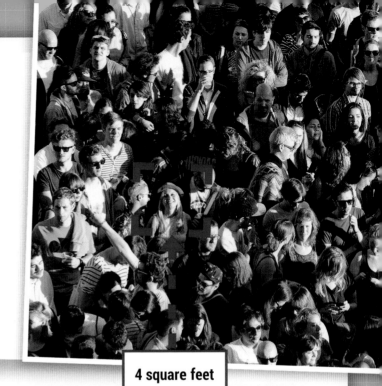

4 square feet

Area of a Triangle

Two identical triangles put together make a parallelogram. The area of a parallelogram is its length times its height. The area of each triangle is half the parallelogram's area. So, the area of a triangle is half the length of its base times its height.

height

base

The area of a triangle is half the length of its base times its height.

Measuring Different Shapes

Some areas look hard to measure. But we can usually take a complicated shape and divide it into simple shapes. We can figure out the areas of the simple shapes. Then we can add them all together to find the area of the whole shape.

Not all rooms in a house are simple squares or rectangles.

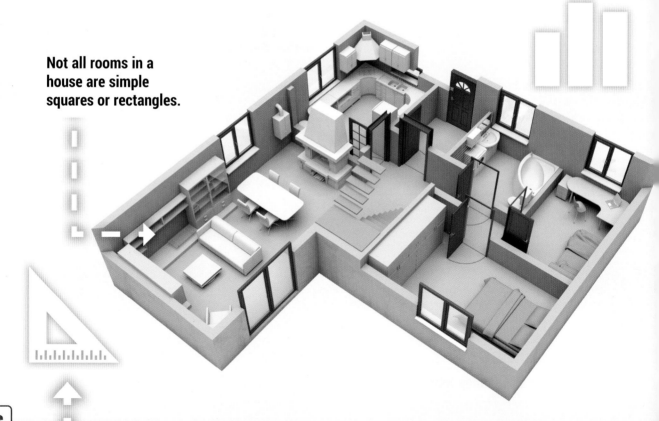

L-SHAPED ROOM

Some rooms are shaped like the letter L. How do you find the area? You can split the L into three rectangles. The area of a rectangle is its length times its width. Find the area of each of the three rectangles. Add them together to get the area of the room.

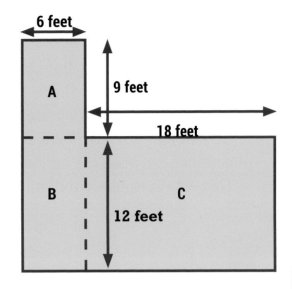

A: 6 feet x 9 feet = 54 square feet

B: 6 feet x 12 feet = 72 square feet

C: 12 feet x 18 feet = 216 square feet

Area of the room =
54 + 72 + 216 = 342 square feet

TRY THIS

FINDING SHAPES

Choose an unusual-shaped room in your home or school. Draw its outline on a piece of paper. Can you divide the room into simpler shapes? Can you figure out the area of the room?

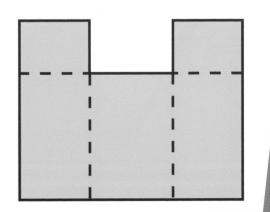

Circle Area

A circle is a round, flat shape. The area of the circle is the space inside the round edge. A circle does not have straight edges that we can measure. How can we estimate the area? We can do this if we know the distance between the center of the circle and the outside. This length is called the radius.

FINDING THE RADIUS

Draw a circle using a compass. Measure the radius. Now we can estimate the area using this: **3 x r x r**, where r is the number you measured for the radius.

For the circle on the left, that is

3 x 2 x 2 = 12 square inches.

Remember that an estimate is a good guess. It isn't an exact answer. And don't forget to add the units!

radius (r) = 2 inches

MAGIC NUMBER

To find the exact area of a circle, we use a special number called **pi**. The number is often written like this, π. Pi is the number 3.141.

To figure out the exact area of a circle with a radius of 4 inches, do this (your answer should be in square inches):

3.141 x r x r = area

You will need to use a calculator!

The answer is on page 32.

FACT

Pi even has its own day! Pi Day is celebrated on March 14 (3/14) each year around the world.

3D Areas

Three-dimensional shapes have an area. Planet Earth is round, like an orange. Round objects are called spheres. The part of the sphere that we see is its outer surface. The surface has an area. It's called the surface area. Earth doesn't seem round when we walk on it. That's because it's so big. We do not notice that Earth is round until we see photographs of it taken from space.

Earth photographed from space.

Square Faces

A cube is a 3D shape with six faces. The faces are all the same size. If we flatten a cube, we can see the six faces. Each face is a square. We can work out the area of each face by multiplying its height by its width. Then we can add all the areas together to find the surface area of the cube.

Dice are cubes.

TRY THIS

SURFACE AREA OF A CUBE

A cube has six identical faces. If the height of a cube is 2 inches, can you find the total surface area? Remember, the area of each face is its height times its width. And there are six faces in the cube.

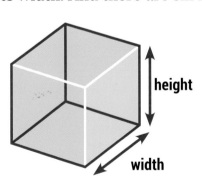

height

width

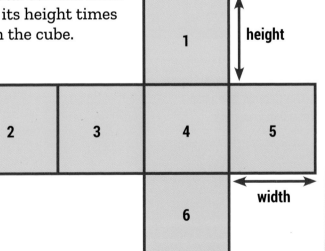

1

height

2 3 4 5

width

6

The answer is on page 32.

Planning with Areas

Knowing about area is useful in everyday life. Farmers need to know how much seed to plant in their fields. One way to do this is to measure the area of a field. Then they can figure out how many plants will fit in the field and how much seed to buy.

Construction sites use large areas of land. People figure out the size of the area before work begins.

Areas can help at home. They can help you figure out how much icing to put on a birthday cake. If you are wrapping a present, you need to know how much paper you need before you start. If you know the size, or area, of the present, you can figure out how much wrapping paper to use.

FACT

Construction teams use special electronic equipment. It can measure the length and height of things very accurately.

Planning Ahead

Area is important for building work. If people are planning a new theme park, they need to know how much space it will take up. They use maps and photographs to help them plan. By figuring out the area, they know how much land they need. They can tell how much material they need for the building work and how much it will cost.

Area from Above

What's the biggest area you can think of measuring? A house? A city? What about measuring the area of a country? Countries are big. And they don't come in standard shapes, like rectangles, squares, or triangles. How do people measure them?

Eye in the Sky

Larger areas are best measured from the sky. People use a photograph of the ground taken from high up in an airplane. This kind of photograph is called an aerial photograph.

On an aerial photograph, buildings, fields, and whole cities look like squares and other simple shapes. If we measure their areas on the photograph, we can figure out their real areas by scaling up.

An aerial photograph of New York City shows buildings and a park.

SCALING UP

Suppose we have an aerial photograph of a park that we know the area of. We can measure the area of the park on the photograph.

The park takes up 1 square inch on the photograph. In real life, the park is 1 acre. So we know that 1 square inch on the photograph is the same as 1 acre of real land.

A different park on the photograph measures 12 square inches. Its real size must be 12 times 1 acre, or 12 acres:

12 x 1 = 12 acres

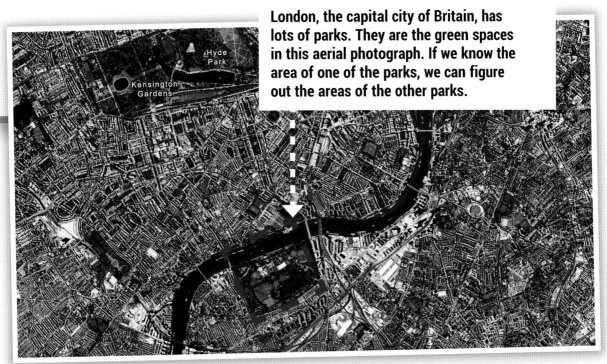

London, the capital city of Britain, has lots of parks. They are the green spaces in this aerial photograph. If we know the area of one of the parks, we can figure out the areas of the other parks.

Area from Space

Satellites move around Earth high up in space. They take pictures of our planet and send them back to scientists. Photographs from space show a lot of information that we can't see on Earth.

Satellite photographs show that seven-tenths of Earth is covered by water. Satellite photographs also show us the areas of the continents. They show how much of Earth's area is farmland and how much is covered by towns and cities.

Satellite photographs show that much of our planet is covered with water. People sometimes call Earth the Blue Planet.

RAIN FORESTS

Rain forests are important for the planet. Trees soak up carbon dioxide gas. This is one of the gases that cause global warming. Satellite photographs show that Earth's rain forests are disappearing. People are cutting them down for farms and roads. Scientists use satellite photographs to measure the area covered by forests. The rain forests get smaller every year as more are destroyed.

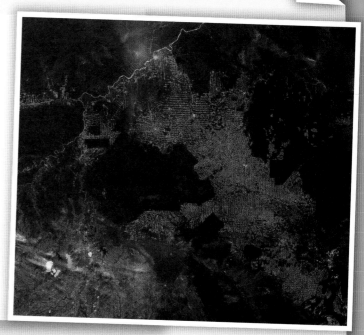

FACT

Since 1988, 10,000 acres (40 square km) of Amazon rain forest has been destroyed every day.

Area and Global Warming

Scientists use satellite photographs to study global warming. That is the way Earth is slowly warming up because of things people do, such as burning coal and gas. Satellite photographs show the area of ice at the North Pole is slowly getting smaller. That shows Earth is heating up. Studying areas is one way we can help save our planet.

Measure Your Room

WHAT YOU NEED

* Large packet of paper
* Ruler
* Pencil

WHAT YOU DO

1. Measure the area of one piece of paper. First measure its height, then measure its width in inches. Multiply the numbers to find the area. Write down your answer. Remember to note the units.

this May Help

Make sure the edges of the paper touch, but don't let the pieces cover each other. Try to cover the floor completely so that all you can see is paper. There may be parts of the floor that you cannot cover. Leave those areas.

2. Carefully cover the floor of your room with pieces of paper. Make sure the pieces touch each other but don't overlap.

3. When the floor is covered as completely as possible, count how many pieces of paper there are.

4. Multiply this number by the area of the first sheet that you measured. The number you get is an estimate of the area of your room in square inches.

Can you think of other ways to measure the area of your room? How do the results compare?

Glossary

area The amount of space taken up by the surface of something.

estimate A rough measurement.

length The distance between two points, usually measured in a straight line.

map A plan of some part of Earth. A map is drawn as though from high up looking down.

parallel lines Straight lines that are always the same distance apart.

parallelogram A four-sided shape in which every side is parallel to the opposite side.

perimeter The distance around the edge of a shape.

pi A number used to figure out areas of circles. It is often written as the symbol π.

radius The distance from the center of a circle to the edge.

rectangle A four-sided shape with right-angled corners.

right angle The angle made by two lines meeting at 90 degrees, such as at the corner of a square.

satellite An uncrewed spacecraft that moves around Earth.

scale up To figure out how big something is from looking at a map.

square unit A measurement of area. Square feet and square inches are examples of square units.

surface area The area that covers the surface of an object.

unit A measurement of something. Examples of units are inches and yards.

Find Out More

BOOKS

Askew, Mike.
Let's Measure It. You Can Master Math.
Rosen Publishing, 2022.

Happy Turtle.
Measure the Rectangle.
Happy Turtle Press, 2020.

Jones, Christianne.
Measuring At Home.
Capstone Publishing, 2019.

Luz, Oscar.
Payton's Plane Figures: Understand Concepts of Area (Math Masters: Measurement and Data).
PowerKids Press, 2015.

WEBSITES

www.mathsisfun.com/geometry/area.html
Simple explanation of area, with clear, useful examples illustrated.

www.splashlearn.com/math/area-games
Games and videos for kids on area and shapes.

www.splashlearn.com/math-vocabulary/geometry/area
The concept of area explained, with many examples and illustrations.

www.twinkl.co.uk/teaching-wiki/area
All about how to work out the areas of different shapes, with examples.

Index

ANSWERS

Page 6: 20 square feet and 64 square feet. **Page 10:** 150 square feet and 64 square inches. **Page 12:** 360,000 square feet. **Page 19:** 50.27 square inches. **Page 21:** 24 square inches.